WRAP
COOKBOOK

Easy Sandwich Wrap Recipes for Beginners

Les Ilagan

TABLE OF CONTENTS

INTRODUCTION

Sandwiches are fun to eat, not to mention that they are delicious and satisfying too. One way to prepare your sandwiches at home is by putting all your filling ingredients into a flatbread like a tortilla or a pita wrap.

Sandwich wraps are good to have for breakfast, snack, lunch, or dinner. And they also make a perfect grab and go food when you are running late for school or work. You only need to put everything together, place it in your lunchbox, and then you are ready to go.

This book offers a wide variety of sandwich wrap recipes that you can choose from. Surely, you will find something here that would best suit your taste and that will also satisfy your cravings.

Most of the recipes here were made simple so that you can easily prepare them at home. While some would require a few cooking skills, you will surely enjoy making them with easy-to-follow instructions.

To many of us, especially the mothers, planning meals that are easy, tasty, and healthy could be a very challenging task. This recipe book will provide you with many delightful meal ideas that you can prepare in a snap.

So, let's get started!

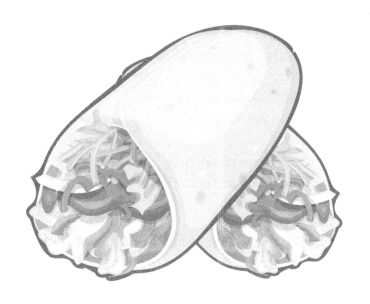

WRAP
RECIPES

TUNA SALAD WRAP

Preparation Time	Total Time	Yield
10 minutes	10 minutes	4 servings

INGREDIENTS

- 1 (6 oz. or 185 g) canned tuna flakes, liquid drained
- 2 (60 g) stalk celery, chopped
- 1/2 cup (125 g) reduced-fat mayonnaise
- 1/4 cup (15 g) chives, chopped
- 1 medium (200 g) cucumber, thinly sliced
- 1 medium (125 g) tomato, thinly sliced
- 4 (6-inch) whole wheat flour tortillas, toasted and warmed
- 8 (20 g) Romaine lettuce leaves
- Salt and freshly ground black pepper

METHOD

- Mix together the tuna, mayonnaise, chopped celery, and chives in a small bowl. Season to taste.
- Put 2 lettuce leaves in the center of each tortilla.
- Spoon about 2-3 tablespoons of tuna mixture and place over lettuce. Top with cucumber and tomato slices. Roll it up to enclose filling.
- Cut in half and serve.
- Enjoy.

NUTRITIONAL INFORMATION

Energy	Fat	Carbohydrates	Protein	Sodium
326 calories	14.5 g	33.9 g	16.6 g	518 mg

HOMEMADE BEEF SHAWARMA WRAP

Preparation Time	Total Time	Yield
20 minutes	1 hour 20 minutes	4 servings

INGREDIENTS

- 1/4 cup (60 ml) olive oil
- 1/4 cup (60 ml) lemon juice
- 3 cloves (10 g) garlic, minced
- 1 teaspoon (2 g) curry powder
- 1/2 teaspoon (1 g) cumin, ground
- 1/2 teaspoon (2.5 g) kosher salt
- 1/4 teaspoon (0.5 g) ground black pepper
- 1 pound (450 g) lean sirloin beef, sliced thinly
- 2 (125 g) tomatoes, chopped
- 1 medium (110 g) onion, sliced thinly
- 2 tablespoons (7 g) fresh cilantro, chopped
- 4 (6-inch) toasted and warmed pita bread

Shawarma sauce:

- 3 (3 g) cloves garlic, minced
- 1/4 cup (80 g) tahini
- 1/2 cup (125 ml) cold water
- 2 tablespoons (30 ml) lemon juice
- 1/2 teaspoon fresh parsley, chopped
- Salt and ground black pepper

METHOD

- Combine the olive oil, lemon juice, garlic, curry, and cumin in a medium glass bowl. Season to taste.
- Add the beef slices and marinate for at least an hour.
- Preheat your grill to medium-high heat.

- Arrange beef slices on the grill and cook for 5-6 minutes on each side or to desired doneness. Cut into thin strips.
- For the Shawarma Sauce: combine the garlic and tahini in a food processor. Turn on the machine and slowly add the cold water along with lemon juice. Add in parsley and season to taste.
- Serve beef strips on pita bread topped with sliced tomatoes, onion, and cilantro. Drizzle with prepared Shawarma sauce. Roll it up to enclose filling.
- Enjoy.

NUTRITIONAL INFORMATION

Energy	Fat	Carbohydrates	Protein	Sodium
454 calories	16.4 g	41.5 g	33.7 g	539 mg

BEEF BURRITO WRAP

Preparation Time	Total Time	Yield
10 minutes	20 minutes	4 servings

INGREDIENTS

- 3 tablespoons (45 ml) olive oil, divided
- 1 pound (450 g) lean beef, minced
- 2 cloves (6 g) garlic, chopped
- 1 medium (110 g) onion, sliced thinly
- 1/2 medium (60 g) green bell pepper, coarsely chopped
- 1/2 medium (60 g) red bell pepper, coarsely chopped
- 1 cup (165 g) frozen sweetcorn kernels, thawed
- 1/2 cup (125 g) canned refried beans
- 1/2 teaspoon (1 g) cumin, ground
- 1/2 teaspoon (1 g) cayenne pepper
- 1/2 teaspoon (1 g) sweet paprika
- 2 tablespoons (7 g) fresh coriander leaves, chopped
- Kosher salt and freshly ground black pepper
- 4 (60 g) whole wheat flour tortillas, toasted and warmed

METHOD

- In a non-stick pan or skillet, add 1 tablespoon oil and heat over medium-high flame. Cook minced beef until browned. Then, transfer to a clean plate and set aside.
- In the same pan, put the remaining 2 tablespoons oil and heat over medium-high flame. Add the onion and garlic; stir-fry until fragrant, about 2-3 minutes.
- Stir in green and red peppers, sweetcorn, refried beans, cumin, cayenne pepper, and paprika. Cook,

stirring for 5 minutes.
- Next, add the beef along with the coriander; cook 2-3 minutes more. Season to taste. Remove from heat. Cool for 10 minutes.
- Divide beef mixture among 4 tortillas. Roll it up to enclose filling.
- Serve and enjoy.

NUTRITIONAL INFORMATION

Energy	Fat	Carbohydrates	Protein	Sodium
378 calories	17.2 g	30.8 g	31.3 g	318 mg

BEEF FAJITA WRAP

Preparation Time	Total Time	Yield
20 minutes	1 hour 20 minutes	8 servings

INGREDIENTS

Marinade:

- 2 tablespoons (30 ml) olive oil
- 2 tablespoons (30 ml) lime juice
- 1 teaspoon (3 g) minced garlic
- 2 teaspoons (4 g) Fajita seasoning

Beef Fajita:

- 2.2 pounds (1 kg) lean beef, cut into thin strips
- 2 tablespoons (30 ml) olive oil, divided
- 2 (110 g) red onion, thinly sliced
- 1 medium (120 g) red bell pepper, chopped
- 1/4 cup (15 g) fresh cilantro, chopped
- 2 tablespoons (30 ml) lime juice
- Kosher salt and freshly ground black pepper
- 8 (60 g) flour tortillas, toasted and warmed
- Guacamole, to serve
- Fresh salsa, to serve
- Lime wedges, to serve

METHOD

- Mix together the ingredients for the marinade in a non-reactive shallow dish. Stir in beef strips and let sit for at least 1 hour.
- In a non-stick pan or skillet add 1 tablespoon oil and heat over medium-high flame. Add the onion and bell pepper. Stir-fry for 3-4 minutes or until softened.

Transfer to a plate. Cover to keep warm.

- Reduce heat to medium. Add remaining oil in the skillet and cook the marinated beef for 3-5 minutes or to your desired doneness.
- Stir in onion mixture, chopped cilantro, and lime juice. Season to taste.
- Divide the stir-fried beef and vegetables among tortillas. Roll to enclose filling.
- Serve with guacamole, salsa, and lime wedges.

NUTRITIONAL INFORMATION

Energy	Fat	Carbohydrates	Protein	Sodium
423 calories	20.9 g	30.5 g	30.1 g	330 mg

SPICED CHICKEN AND PEPPER WRAP

Preparation Time	Total Time	Yield
10 minutes	25 minutes	4 servings

INGREDIENTS

- 2 tablespoons (30 ml) canola oil
- 1 medium (110 g) onion, chopped
- 2 cloves (6 g) garlic, minced
- 1 pound (450 g) chicken thigh fillet, diced
- 1 medium (120 g) red bell pepper, chopped
- 1 tablespoon (15 ml) soy sauce
- 1 tablespoon (15 ml) Worcestershire sauce
- 1 teaspoon (2 g) cayenne pepper
- 1 teaspoon (2 g) paprika
- 1 teaspoon (2 g) cumin, ground
- 4 (60 g) whole wheat tortillas, toasted and warmed

METHOD

- Add 2 tablespoons oil in a skillet or pan over medium-high flame. Add the chopped onion and garlic; cook, stirring often for 3 minutes.
- Add the diced chicken and cook until browned.
- Add the bell pepper, soy sauce, Worcestershire sauce, cayenne pepper, paprika, and cumin. Cook, stirring for another 3-5 minutes. Remove from heat and cool slightly.
- Divide the stir-fried chicken and pepper mixture among 4 warmed tortillas. Roll it up to enclose filling.

- Serve and enjoy.

NUTRITIONAL INFORMATION

Energy	Fat	Carbohydrates	Protein	Sodium
400 calories	10.9 g	40.2 g	34.1 g	551 mg

CHICKEN AUBERGINE TOMATO AND ROCKET WRAP

Preparation Time	Total Time	Yield
10 minutes	1 hour 25 minutes	5 servings

INGREDIENTS

- 4 tablespoons (60 ml) olive oil, divided
- 2 tablespoons (30 ml) lemon juice
- 2 teaspoons (6 g) garlic, minced
- 1/2 teaspoon (1 g) coriander seed, ground
- 1/2 teaspoon (2.5 g) Kosher salt
- 1/4 teaspoon (0.5 g) ground black pepper
- 1 pound (450 g) skinless chicken breast fillet, thinly sliced
- 1 pound (450 g) aubergine (eggplant), thinly sliced
- 1 medium (110 g) red onion, sliced thinly
- 2 cups (60 g) baby rocket leaves (arugula)
- 2 (125 g) tomatoes, thinly sliced
- 5 (60 g) whole wheat flour tortillas, toasted and warmed
- Choice of salad dressing, to serve

METHOD

- In a medium non-reactive bowl, mix together 2 tablespoons olive oil, lemon juice, garlic, ground coriander, salt, and pepper. Add the chicken slices. Cover and let it sit in the refrigerator for at least an hour.
- Preheat your grill or griddle to high heat.

- Place marinated chicken on the grill. Cook for about 7-8 minutes on each side or until cooked through and grill marks form. Cut into thin strips.
- Drizzle aubergine and onion with remaining 2 tablespoons olive oil. Season with some salt and pepper. Grill the vegetables on both sides until softened and grill marks form.
- Divide the grilled chicken and vegetables among 5 warmed tortillas. Drizzle with your choice of dressing. Roll to enclose filling.
- Serve and enjoy.

NUTRITIONAL INFORMATION

Energy	Fat	Carbohydrates	Protein	Sodium
368 calories	14.6 g	40.1 g	29.7 g	529 mg

SHRIMP EGG AND VEGGIE WRAP

Preparation Time	Total Time	Yield
10 minutes	10 minutes	4 servings

INGREDIENTS

- 2 (60 g) hard-boiled eggs, sliced thinly
- 1 pound (450 g) steamed shrimps, peeled
- 1 medium (110 g) white onion, sliced thinly
- 1 medium (125 g) tomato, thinly sliced
- 1/2 cup (125 g) ranch dressing
- 4 (60 g) whole wheat flour tortillas, toasted and warmed
- 8 (20 g) lettuce leaves

METHOD

- Arrange 2 lettuce leaves at the center of each tortilla. Top with shrimps, egg, onion, and tomato.
- Drizzle with 2 tablespoons ranch dressing. Roll the warmed tortillas to enclose the shrimp filling.
- Serve and enjoy.

NUTRITIONAL INFORMATION

Energy	Fat	Carbohydrates	Protein	Sodium
381 calories	11.1 g	46.9 g	23.6 g	572 mg

CHICKEN AND VEGETABLE WRAP WITH HONEY MUSTARD SAUCE

Preparation Time	Total Time	Yield
10 minutes	10 minutes	4 servings

INGREDIENTS

- 1 pound (450 g) grilled chicken fillet, cut into small strips
- 1 medium (110 g) red onion, sliced thinly
- 1 medium (120 g) yellow bell pepper, sliced thinly
- 1 medium (125 g) tomato, sliced thinly
- 2 cups (60 g) baby rocket or arugula
- 4 (60 g) whole wheat flour tortillas, toasted and warmed

Honey-Mustard Sauce:

- 1/3 cup (85 g) light mayonnaise
- 2 tablespoons (30 g) Dijon mustard
- 2 tablespoons (40 ml) honey
- Salt and freshly ground black pepper

METHOD

- In a small bowl, combine the mayonnaise, Dijon mustard, and honey. Mix thoroughly and season to taste.
- Divide the chicken strips and vegetables among 4 tortillas. Drizzle with honey-mustard sauce. Roll it up to enclose the filling.

- Serve and enjoy.

NUTRITIONAL INFORMATION

Energy	Fat	Carbohydrates	Protein	Sodium
422 calories	10.1 g	50.4 g	31.8 g	651 mg

EASY CHICKEN FAJITA WRAP

Preparation Time	Total Time	Yield
10 minutes	1 hour 25 minutes	8 servings

INGREDIENTS

Marinade:

- 2 tablespoons (30 ml) olive oil
- 2 tablespoons (30 ml) lemon juice
- 2 (3 g) cloves garlic, minced
- 2 teaspoons (4 g) Fajita seasoning

Chicken Fajita:

- 2.2 pounds (1 kg) chicken fillet, cut into thin strips
- 2 tablespoons (30 ml) olive oil
- 1 medium (110 g) onion, sliced thinly
- 1 medium (120 g) red bell pepper, sliced thinly
- 1 medium (120 g) green bell pepper, sliced thinly
- 2 tablespoons (7 g) fresh cilantro, coarsely chopped
- 1 tablespoon (15 ml) Worcestershire sauce
- 2 tablespoons (30 ml) lemon juice
- 8 (60 g) whole wheat tortillas
- Guacamole, to serve
- Fresh salsa, to serve
- Lemon wedges, to serve

METHOD

- In a shallow dish, combine the marinade ingredients. Stir in chicken strips and marinate for an hour.
- Heat 1 tablespoon oil in a large skillet over medium-

high flame. Add the onion and bell pepper. Cook for 2-3 minutes or until softened. Transfer to a plate. Cover to keep warm.

- Heat remaining oil and cook the chicken strips until browned.
- Stir in onion mixture, cilantro, Worcestershire sauce, and lemon juice. Cook further 3-5 minutes. Remove from heat and season to taste.
- Heat the tortillas following the package instructions.
- Serve chicken and vegetable sauté on tortilla wrap with fresh salsa and guacamole.
- Enjoy.

NUTRITIONAL INFORMATION

Energy	Fat	Carbohydrates	Protein	Sodium
428 calories	22.3 g	25.6 g	30.7 g	627 mg

CHICKEN HAM EGG AND CHEESE WRAP

Preparation Time	Total Time	Yield
10 minutes	15 minutes	4 servings

INGREDIENTS

- 4 (60 g) large eggs
- 2 (40 g) egg whites
- 1/4 cup (60 ml) skim milk
- 2 tablespoons (30 ml) canola oil
- 4 ounces (125 g) chicken ham, chopped
- 1/4 cup (30 g) cheddar cheese, grated
- 2 tablespoons (7 g) fresh parsley, chopped
- 1/4 teaspoon (0.5 g) ground black pepper
- 4 (60 g) whole wheat flour tortillas, toasted and warmed

METHOD

- Beat together the eggs and milk in a medium bowl. Set aside.
- Heat oil in a skillet over medium-high flame. Add the chicken ham; cook, stirring for a couple of minutes.
- Add the beaten egg-milk mixture and cook for 2-3 minutes, stirring often.
- Add the cheese and parsley. Cook further 2 minutes, stirring often. Season with pepper to taste. Remove from heat and cool slightly.
- Divide the egg mixture among 4 warmed tortillas. Roll it up to enclose filling.
- Serve and enjoy.

NUTRITIONAL INFORMATION

Energy	Fat	Carbohydrates	Protein	Sodium
324 calories	18.5 g	18.3 g	21.4 g	616 mg

GREEK-STYLE CHICKEN WRAP

Preparation Time	Total Time	Yield
10 minutes	10 minutes	4 servings

INGREDIENTS

- 1 pound (450 g) roasted or baked chicken fillet, cut into strips
- 1 cup (125 g) cherry tomatoes, quartered
- 8 (8 g) pitted black olives, sliced
- 1/2 cup (125 g) feta cheese, crumbled
- 1 cup (60 g) fresh basil leaves
- 4 (60 g) whole wheat flour tortillas, toasted and warmed

Yogurt-Herb Dressing:

- 6 oz. (185 g) Greek yogurt, plain
- 1 tablespoon (3.5 g) fresh parsley, chopped
- 1 teaspoon (3 g) garlic, minced
- Salt and freshly ground black pepper

METHOD

- In a small bowl, mix together yogurt, parsley, and garlic. Mix well and season to taste. Set aside.
- Divide the chicken strips, tomatoes, olives, feta cheese, and basil among 4 warmed tortillas. Drizzle with yogurt dressing. Roll tortillas to enclose filling. Cut them in half crosswise.
- Serve and enjoy.

NUTRITIONAL INFORMATION

Energy	Fat	Carbohydrates	Protein	Sodium
335 calories	13.7 g	20.9 g	31.2 g	557 mg

CHICKEN MANGO AND TOMATO WRAP

Preparation Time	Total Time	Yield
10 minutes	10 minutes	4 servings

INGREDIENTS

- 1 pound (450 g) roasted chicken breast fillet, cut into thin strips
- 1 cup (165 g) mango, diced
- 2 (125 g) tomatoes, diced
- 2 tablespoons (7 g) fresh parsley, chopped
- Salt and freshly ground black pepper
- 4 (60 g) whole wheat flour tortillas, toasted and warmed

Dressing:

- 1/2 cup (125 g) light mayonnaise
- 2 tablespoons (30 g) Dijon mustard

METHOD

- Mix together the mayonnaise and Dijon mustard. Set aside.
- Combine the chicken, mango, tomatoes, and parsley in a medium bowl. Season to taste. Mix thoroughly.
- Divide the mixture among 4 tortillas. Drizzle with dressing. Roll it up to enclose filling.
- Serve and enjoy.

NUTRITIONAL INFORMATION

Energy	Fat	Carbohydrates	Protein	Sodium
368 calories	14.4 g	34.9 g	24.8 g	580 mg

BEEF AND VEGGIE WRAP

Preparation Time	Total Time	Yield
10 minutes	25 minutes	4 servings

INGREDIENTS

- 1 pound (450 g) beef sirloin, cut into thin strips
- 1 teaspoon (2 g) cumin, ground
- 1/2 teaspoon (2.5 g) kosher salt
- 1/4 teaspoon (0.5 g) ground black pepper
- 2 tablespoons (30 ml) olive oil, divided
- 2 teaspoons (6 g) garlic, crushed
- 2 medium tomatoes (about 125 g each), sliced thinly
- 1/2 medium (60 g) red bell pepper, sliced thinly
- 1/2 medium (60 g) green bell pepper, sliced thinly
- 1 medium (110 g) red onion, sliced thinly
- 4 (60 g) whole wheat flour tortillas, toasted and warmed
- 8 (20 g) lettuce leaves

METHOD

- Season beef with cumin, salt, and pepper. Set aside.
- Heat 1 tablespoon oil in a medium skillet over medium-high flame. Cook the beef strips for 3-5 minutes or until browned. Transfer to a clean plate.
- Using the same skillet, heat remaining oil. Stir fry garlic until fragrant, about 1 minute.
- Add the tomato and bell pepper slices. Cook, stirring for about 3-5 minutes.
- Add the beef and onion. Cook further 2-3 minutes.

Remove from heat and cool slightly.

- Divide the beef and vegetable mixture among 4 warmed tortillas. Roll it up to enclose filling.
- Serve and enjoy.

NUTRITIONAL INFORMATION

Energy	Fat	Carbohydrates	Protein	Sodium
374 calories	15.7 g	28.2 g	20.8 g	465 mg

CHICKEN TIKKA WRAP

Preparation Time	Total Time	Yield
10 minutes	10 minutes	4 servings

INGREDIENTS

- 1 pound (450 g) leftover chicken tikka, cut into small pieces
- 1 medium (200 g) cucumber, sliced thinly
- 1 medium (110 g) onion, sliced thinly
- 1 cup (50 g) iceberg lettuce, shredded
- 1/4 cup (15 g) scallions, chopped
- 2 tablespoons (30 ml) lime juice
- 6 ounces (185 g) plain yogurt
- 4 (60 g) pita bread, toasted and warmed
- Salt and freshly ground black pepper

METHOD

- Mix together the leftover chicken tikka, cucumber, onion, lettuce, and scallions in a medium bowl. Add 2 tablespoons lime juice and season to taste. Toss to combine well.
- Divide the chicken and vegetable mixture among 4 pita bread. Drizzle with yogurt. Then, roll it up to enclose filling.
- Serve and enjoy.

NUTRITIONAL INFORMATION

Energy	Fat	Carbohydrates	Protein	Sodium
332 calories	6.5 g	44.6 g	25.3 g	569 mg

CRISPY CHICKEN SALAD WRAP

Preparation Time	Total Time	Yield
10 minutes	35 minutes	4 servings

INGREDIENTS

- 1 pound (450 g) chicken breast fillet, cut into 3-inch sticks
- Salt and freshly ground black pepper
- 3/4 cup (90 g) all-purpose flour
- 3/4 cup (185 ml) milk
- 3/4 cup (75 g) breadcrumbs
- 1 medium (125 g) tomato, thinly sliced
- 1 medium (200 g) cucumber, thinly sliced
- 8 (20 g) Romaine lettuce leaves
- 4 (60 g) whole wheat flour tortillas, toasted and warmed
- Cooking oil spray
- Choice of dressing, to serve

METHOD

- Preheat and set your oven to 400 F (200 C).
- Season chicken sticks with salt and pepper. Dredge with flour, dip in milk, and then roll in breadcrumbs. Place in a baking sheet to make a single layer. Spray with oil.
- Bake chicken in the oven for 20 to 25 minutes or until golden brown and cooked through. Remove from heat. Cool slightly.
- Divide the chicken sticks, tomato, cucumber, and lettuce among 4 warmed tortillas. Drizzle with your

choice of dressing. Roll it up to enclose filling.

• Serve and enjoy.

NUTRITIONAL INFORMATION

Energy	Fat	Carbohydrates	Protein	Sodium
350 calories	7.5 g	43.4 g	27.2 g	450 mg

FISH FILLET CHEESE AND LETTUCE WRAP

Preparation Time	Total Time	Yield
10 minutes	35 minutes	4 servings

INGREDIENTS

- 1 pound (450 g) fish fillet, cut into 3-inch sticks
- Salt and freshly ground black pepper
- 3/4 cup (90 g) all-purpose flour
- 3/4 cup (185 ml) milk
- 3/4 cup (75 g) breadcrumbs
- 2 (125 g) tomatoes, thinly sliced
- 1 medium (200 g) cucumber, thinly sliced
- 4 slices cheddar cheese, about 2 oz. or 30 g each
- 8 (20 g) Romaine lettuce leaves
- 4 (60 g) whole wheat flour tortillas, toasted and warmed
- Cooking oil spray
- Choice of dressing, to serve

METHOD

- Preheat and set your oven to 400 F (200 C).
- Season fish sticks with salt and pepper. Dredge with flour, dip in milk, and then roll in breadcrumbs. Place in a baking sheet to make a single layer. Spray with oil.
- Bake fish in the oven for about 18-20 minutes or until golden brown and cooked through. Remove from heat. Cool slightly.
- Divide the baked fish sticks, tomato slices, cheddar cheese, and lettuce among 4 tortillas. Drizzle with your

choice of dressing. Roll it up to enclose filling.
- Serve and enjoy.

NUTRITIONAL INFORMATION

Energy	Fat	Carbohydrates	Protein	Sodium
385 calories	21.2 g	28.7 g	21.9 g	585 mg

EASY BREAKFAST WRAP

Preparation Time	Total Time	Yield
10 minutes	15 minutes	4 servings

INGREDIENTS

- 4 (60 g) large eggs
- 2 (40 g) egg whites
- 2 tablespoons (30 g) light mayonnaise
- 2 tablespoons (30 ml) canola oil
- 1 medium (110 g) white onion, chopped
- 2 medium tomatoes (about 125 g each), chopped
- 2 tablespoons (7 g) fresh parsley, chopped
- 1/2 cup (60 g) cheddar cheese, grated
- 4 (60 g) whole wheat flour tortillas, toasted and warmed
- Salt and freshly ground black pepper

METHOD

- Beat together the eggs and mayonnaise in a medium bowl. Set aside.
- Heat 2 tablespoons oil in a skillet over medium-high flame. Stir-fry onion and tomatoes for 2-3 minutes or until softened.
- Pour the egg mixture and parsley. Cook, stirring for 3-4 minutes. Season with salt and pepper to taste. Remove from heat and cool slightly.
- Divide the scrambled eggs among 4 warmed tortillas. Sprinkle with cheddar cheese. Roll it up to enclose filling.

- Serve and enjoy.

NUTRITIONAL INFORMATION

Energy	Fat	Carbohydrates	Protein	Sodium
348 calories	22.2 g	25.7 g	13.1 g	460 mg

FALAFEL WRAP WITH TARATOR SAUCE

Preparation Time	Total Time	Yield
15 minutes	15 minutes	4 servings

INGREDIENTS

- 8 (20 g) small falafel balls, cooked
- 2 cups (60 g) arugula or baby rocket leaves
- 1 (200 g) Lebanese cucumber, thinly sliced
- 1 medium (125 g) tomato, thinly sliced
- 4 (60 g) pita bread, toasted and warmed

Tarator Sauce:

- 1/2 cup (125 g) tahini paste
- 1/2 cup (125 ml) water
- 1/4 cup (60 ml) lemon juice
- 1/2 teaspoon (1.5 g) garlic, minced
- 1 teaspoon (1 g) fresh parsley, chopped
- Salt and freshly ground black pepper

METHOD

- In a small mixing bowl, combine all ingredients for the Tarator Sauce. Mix well and season to taste.
- Divide the falafel balls, arugula, cucumber, and tomato among 4 pita bread.
- Drizzle with prepared Tarator sauce. Roll it up to enclose filling.
- Serve and enjoy.

NUTRITIONAL INFORMATION

Energy	Fat	Carbohydrates	Protein	Sodium
299 calories	9.1 g	44.5 g	12.3 g	296 mg

VEGETARIAN WRAP WITH CHEDDAR CHEESE

Preparation Time	Total Time	Yield
10 minutes	10 minutes	4 servings

INGREDIENTS

- 2 medium (60 g) carrot, cut into strips
- 1 medium (125 g) tomato, cut into strips
- 1 medium (200 g) cucumber, cut into strips
- 1 medium (120 g) bell pepper, cut into strips
- 1/2 cup (20 g) sweet basil leaves
- 8 oz. (250 g) cheddar cheese, sliced
- 4 (60 g) whole wheat tortillas, toasted and warmed

METHOD

- Divide the carrot, tomato, cucumber, bell pepper basil, and cheddar among 4 tortillas. Roll it up to enclose filling.
- Serve and enjoy.

NUTRITIONAL INFORMATION

Energy	Fat	Carbohydrates	Protein	Sodium
255 calories	11.2 g	27.1 g	12.2 g	438 mg

EASY VEGGIE WRAP

Preparation Time	Total Time	Yield
15 minutes	15 minutes	4 servings

INGREDIENTS

- 1 cup (165 g) canned sweetcorn kernels, drained
- 1 cup (125 g) cherry tomatoes, quartered
- 1 medium (200 g) cucumber, thinly sliced
- 1 medium (110 g) onion, thinly sliced
- 2 tablespoons (30 ml) olive oil
- 2 tablespoons (30 ml) lemon juice
- 1 tablespoon (15 ml) honey
- 4 (60 g) flour tortillas, toasted and warmed
- Salt and fresh ground black pepper

METHOD

- In a medium bowl, mix together sweetcorn, tomatoes, cucumber, and onion. Drizzle with olive oil, lemon juice, and honey. Toss to combine well. Season with salt and pepper to taste.
- Divide the vegetable mixture among 4 warmed tortillas. Roll it up to enclose filling.
- Serve and enjoy.

NUTRITIONAL INFORMATION

Energy	Fat	Carbohydrates	Protein	Sodium
266 calories	10.5 g	39.2 g	5.1 g	374 mg

EGG PEPPER AND LETTUCE WRAP

Preparation Time	Total Time	Yield
10 minutes	10 minutes	4 servings

INGREDIENTS

- 4 (60 g) hard-boiled eggs, sliced thinly
- 1 medium (125 g) tomato, sliced thinly
- 1 medium (125 g) red bell pepper, sliced thinly
- 1 medium (125 g) white onion, sliced thinly
- 8 (20 g) Romaine lettuce leaves
- 4 (60 g) whole wheat flour tortillas, toasted and warmed
- 1/2 cup (125 g) ranch dressing

METHOD

- Divide the eggs, tomato, bell pepper, onion, and lettuce among 4 warmed tortillas. Drizzle with ranch dressing. Roll it up to enclose filling.
- Serve and enjoy.

NUTRITIONAL INFORMATION

Energy	Fat	Carbohydrates	Protein	Sodium
277 calories	12.4 g	31.8 g	10.8 g	498 mg

FRESH VEGETARIAN WRAP

Preparation Time	Total Time	Yield
10 minutes	10 minutes	4 servings

INGREDIENTS

- 1 medium (200 g) avocado, stoned and sliced thinly
- 1 medium (125 g) tomato, sliced thinly
- 1 medium (120 g) red bell pepper, sliced thinly
- 1 medium (110 g) red onion, sliced thinly
- 8 (20 g) Romaine lettuce leaves
- 4 (60 g) whole wheat flour tortillas, toasted and warmed
- Choice of dressing, to serve

METHOD

- Divide the avocado, tomato, bell pepper, onion, and lettuce among 4 tortillas. Drizzle with your choice of dressing. Roll it up to enclose filling.
- Serve and enjoy.

NUTRITIONAL INFORMATION

Energy	Fat	Carbohydrates	Protein	Sodium
243 calories	11.0 g	33.8 g	6.0 g	138 mg

MEDITERRANEAN SALAD WRAP

Preparation Time	Total Time	Yield
10 minutes	10 minutes	4 servings

INGREDIENTS

- 8 ounces (250 g) feta cheese, diced
- 1 cup (150 g) cherry tomatoes, halved
- 1 medium (120 g) red bell pepper, sliced thinly into strips
- 1 medium (200 g) cucumber, sliced thinly
- 8 (8 g) black olives, sliced
- 8 (15 g) Romaine lettuce leaves
- 4 (60 g) flour tortillas, toasted and warmed
- 6 ounces (185 g) Greek yogurt, plain

METHOD

- Divide the feta cheese, tomato, bell pepper, cucumber, olives, and lettuce among 4 tortillas. Drizzle with Greek yogurt. Season with salt and pepper to taste. Roll it up to enclose filling.
- Serve and enjoy.

NUTRITIONAL INFORMATION

Energy	Fat	Carbohydrates	Protein	Sodium
332 calories	14.9 g	34.1 g	17.7 g	639 mg

GRILLED CHICKEN MANGO AND AVOCADO WRAP

Preparation Time	Total Time	Yield
10 minutes	10 minutes	4 servings

INGREDIENTS

- 12 ounces (350 g) grilled chicken breast fillet, cut into strips
- 1 medium (200 g) avocado, sliced thinly
- 1 cup (165 g) mango, sliced thinly
- 1 medium (125 g) tomato, sliced thinly
- 1 medium (120 g) red bell pepper, sliced thinly into strips
- 1 medium (110 g) red onion, sliced thinly
- 8 (15 g) Romaine lettuce leaves
- 4 (60 g) flour tortillas, toasted and warmed
- Salt and freshly ground black pepper
- Greek yogurt, to serve

METHOD

- Divide the chicken, avocado, mango, tomato, bell pepper, onion, and lettuce among 4 tortillas. Season to taste.
- Drizzle with yogurt. Roll it up to enclose filling.
- Serve and enjoy.

NUTRITIONAL INFORMATION

Energy	Fat	Carbohydrates	Protein	Sodium
415 calories	16.3 g	45.1 g	25.3 g	294 mg

GRILLED TUNA AND VEGGIE WRAP

Preparation Time	Total Time	Yield
10 minutes	1 hour 20 minutes	4 servings

INGREDIENTS

- 2 tablespoons (30 ml) olive oil
- 2 tablespoons (30 ml) lime juice
- 1 teaspoon (3 g) garlic, minced
- 2 teaspoons (2 g) fresh dill weed, chopped
- 1 pound (450 g) tuna steak
- 1 medium (110 g) red onion, sliced thinly
- 1 medium (125 g) tomato, sliced thinly
- 8 (15 g) Romaine lettuce leaves
- 4 (60 g) flour tortillas, toasted and warmed
- Kosher salt and freshly ground black pepper
- Choice of dressing, to serve

METHOD

- In a shallow non-reactive dish, combine the olive oil, lime juice, garlic, and dill. Add the tuna steak and let sit for at least 1 hour.
- Preheat grill to high.
- Grill the tuna steak to desired doneness and grill marks form. Remove from heat and cut into strips.
- Divide the tuna, onion, tomato and lettuce among 4 tortillas. Season with salt and pepper to taste. Drizzle with your choice of dressing. Roll it up to enclose filling.
- Serve and enjoy.

NUTRITIONAL INFORMATION

Energy	Fat	Carbohydrates	Protein	Sodium
400 calories	17.3 g	22.8 g	37.7 g	311 mg

MEAT AND VEGETABLE WRAP

Preparation Time	Total Time	Yield
10 minutes	25 minutes	4 servings

INGREDIENTS

- 1 tablespoon (15 g) butter
- 1 pound (450 g) beef sirloin, cut into thin strips
- 2 tablespoons (30 ml) olive oil
- 1 medium (110 g) onion, chopped
- 1 teaspoon (3 g) garlic, minced
- 1 medium (60 g) carrot, chopped
- 1 medium (120 g) red bell pepper, cut into strips
- 1/2 cup (125 g) tomato sauce
- 1 tablespoon (15 ml) Worcestershire sauce
- 1 tablespoon (3.5 g) fresh oregano, chopped
- 8 (15 g) Romaine lettuce leaves
- 4 (60 g) whole wheat flour tortillas, toasted and warmed
- Kosher salt and freshly ground black pepper

METHOD

- Melt butter in a non-stick pan or skillet over medium heat. Stir-fry beef until browned. Transfer to a clean plate.
- Using the same pan, heat oil over medium-high heat. Stir-fry onion and garlic for 1-2 minutes.
- Add the carrot and bell pepper. Cook until tender.
- Add the beef, tomato sauce, Worcestershire sauce, and oregano. Cook further 3-5 minutes, stirring often.

Season with salt and pepper to taste. Remove from heat. Cool slightly.
- Place 2 lettuce leaves on each tortilla, then top with beef and veggie mixture. Roll it up to enclose filling.
- Serve and enjoy.

NUTRITIONAL INFORMATION

Energy	Fat	Carbohydrates	Protein	Sodium
347 calories	15.5 g	22.8 g	29.2 g	297 mg

MEXICAN BEEF WRAP

Preparation Time	Total Time	Yield
10 minutes	25 minutes	4 servings

INGREDIENTS

- 2 tablespoons (30 ml) olive oil
- 1 medium (110 g) onion, chopped
- 1 teaspoon (3 g) garlic, minced
- 1 pound (450 g) lean ground beef
- 1/2 cup (85 g) sweet corn kernels
- 1 medium (125 g) red bell pepper, diced
- 1/2 cup (125 g) tomato sauce
- 1 tablespoon (15 g) tomato paste
- 2 tablespoons (7 g) fresh coriander, chopped
- 1/2 teaspoon (1 g) cayenne pepper
- 1/2 teaspoon (1 g) cumin, ground
- 1/2 cup (60 g) cheddar cheese, grated
- 4 (60 g) flour tortillas, toasted and warmed
- Salt and freshly ground black pepper
- Fresh salsa, to serve

METHOD

- Add 2 tablespoons olive oil in a pan or skillet and heat over medium-high flame. Stir-fry onion and garlic until fragrant, about 2-3 minutes.
- Add the beef and stir-fry until browned.
- Add the corn, bell pepper, tomato sauce, tomato paste, coriander, cayenne pepper, and cumin. Cook for another 7-10 minutes, stirring occasionally. Season with salt and pepper to taste. Remove from heat and

cool slightly.

- Divide beef mixture among 4 tortillas. Sprinkle with cheddar cheese. Roll it up to enclose filling.
- Top with fresh salsa.
- Serve and enjoy.

NUTRITIONAL INFORMATION

Energy	Fat	Carbohydrates	Protein	Sodium
380 calories	18.3 g	21.1 g	32.8 g	324 mg

MEXICAN CHICKEN QUESADILLA WRAP

Preparation Time	Total Time	Yield
10 minutes	25 minutes	4 servings

INGREDIENTS

- 2 tablespoons (30 ml) canola oil
- 2 shallots (about 40 g) each), chopped
- 1 teaspoon (3 g) garlic, chopped
- 1 pound (450 g) chicken breast fillet, ground
- 1/2 cup (85 g) sweet corn kernels
- 1 medium (120 g) red bell pepper, chopped
- 1/2 cup (125 g) tomato sauce
- 1 tablespoon (15 g) tomato paste
- 2 tablespoons (7 g) fresh parsley, finely chopped
- 1 teaspoon (2 g) cayenne pepper
- 1 teaspoon (2 g) sweet paprika
- 1 cup (125 g) sharp cheddar cheese, grated
- 8 (60 g) flour tortillas, toasted and warmed
- Salt and freshly ground black pepper

METHOD

- Heat oil in a large pan or skillet over medium-high flame. Stir-fry shallots and garlic until fragrant, about 3 minutes.
- Add the ground chicken and cook for 5 minutes, stirring often.
- Add the corn, bell pepper, tomato sauce, tomato paste, parsley, cayenne pepper, and paprika. Cook

for another 7-10 minutes, stirring occasionally. Season with salt and pepper to taste. Remove from heat and cool slightly.

- Preheat your broiler to 425 F (210 C).
- Place 4 tortillas in a baking sheet. Divide chicken mixture among the tortillas. Sprinkle with cheddar cheese. Top with remaining tortillas.
- Bake in the oven for about 8-10 minutes. Cut each into 4 slices.
- Serve immediately and enjoy.

NUTRITIONAL INFORMATION

Energy	Fat	Carbohydrates	Protein	Sodium
392 calories	19.2 g	29.8 g	26.9 g	544 mg

CHEESY PHILLY STEAK WRAP

Preparation Time	Total Time	Yield
10 minutes	30 minutes	4 servings

INGREDIENTS

- 3 tablespoons (45 ml) canola oil, divided
- 1 pound (450 g) beef sirloin, cut into thin strips
- 3 medium (110 g) onion, sliced thinly
- 8 (60 g) whole wheat flour tortillas, toasted and warmed
- Salt and freshly ground black pepper

Cheese Sauce:

- 2 tablespoons (30 g) butter
- 1 1/2 tablespoons (10 g) plain flour
- 2/3 cup (165 ml) milk
- 1/3 cup (40 g) sharp cheddar cheese, grated
- 2 tablespoons (15 g) mozzarella cheese, shredded
- 1 teaspoon (5 ml) Worcestershire sauce
- 1 teaspoon (5 g) hot English mustard

METHOD

- In a non-stick pan or skillet, add 1 tablespoon oil and place over medium-high flame. Cook beef for 3-5 minutes, stirring often. Season with salt and pepper to taste. Transfer beef strips to a clean plate and cover with foil to keep warm.
- Using the same pan, heat remaining oil over medium heat. Cook onion until translucent and caramelized, stirring frequently. Remove from heat and set aside.

- To make the Cheese Sauce: Melt butter in a small saucepan. Stir in flour; cook, stirring for 1 minute. Stir in the milk and cook for about 2-3 minutes or until thickened. Add the cheddar, mozzarella, Worcestershire sauce, and hot English mustard.
- Divide the beef and caramelized onions among 4 warmed tortillas. Drizzle with cheese sauce. Roll it up to enclose filling.
- Serve immediately and enjoy.

NUTRITIONAL INFORMATION

Energy	Fat	Carbohydrates	Protein	Sodium
496 calories	23.9 g	36.7 g	32.2 g	543 mg

ROASTED TURKEY CHEDDAR AND LETTUCE WRAP

Preparation Time	Total Time	Yield
10 minutes	10 minutes	4 servings

INGREDIENTS

- 1 pound (450 g) roasted turkey breast fillet, thinly sliced
- 2 medium tomatoes (about 120 g each), sliced thinly
- 4 ounces (125 g) cheddar cheese, sliced thinly
- 8 (15 g) Romaine lettuce leaves
- 4 (60 g) whole wheat flour tortillas, toasted and warmed
- 1/4 cup (60 ml) lemon vinaigrette dressing
- Salt and freshly ground black pepper

METHOD

- Divide the turkey, tomato, cheddar, and lettuce leaves among tortillas. Drizzle with lemon vinaigrette and season to taste. Roll it up to enclose filling. Cut into 5 slices crosswise.
- Serve and enjoy.

NUTRITIONAL INFORMATION

Energy	Fat	Carbohydrates	Protein	Sodium
390 calories	18.1 g	28.7 g	27.2 g	323 mg

LEFTOVER ROAST BEEF SANDWICH WRAP

Preparation Time	Total Time	Yield
10 minutes	10 minutes	4 servings

INGREDIENTS

- 1 pound (450 g) leftover roast beef, sliced thinly
- 2 medium tomatoes (about 120 g each), sliced thinly
- 4 ounce (125 g) cheddar cheese, sliced thinly
- 2 cups (60 g) arugula or baby rocket
- 4 (60 g) whole wheat flour tortillas, toasted and warmed
- Salt and freshly ground black pepper
- Choice of dressing, to serve

METHOD

- Divide the roast beef, tomato, cheddar cheese, and arugula among 4 warmed tortillas. Season to taste. Drizzle with your choice of dressing. Roll it up to enclose filling. Cut in half crosswise.
- Serve and enjoy.

NUTRITIONAL INFORMATION

Energy	Fat	Carbohydrates	Protein	Sodium
426 calories	18.8 g	25.9 g	37.2 g	561 mg

CHICKEN HAM VEGGIE AND CHEESE WRAP

Preparation Time	Total Time	Yield
10 minutes	10 minutes	4 servings

INGREDIENTS

- 4 (30 g) thin slices of chicken or turkey ham
- 2 medium tomatoes (about 125 g each), sliced thinly
- 1 medium (60 g) carrot, julienned
- 4 ounces (125 g) cheddar cheese, sliced thinly
- 8 (15 g) iceberg lettuce leaves
- 4 (60 g) whole wheat flour tortillas, toasted and warmed
- Salt and freshly ground black pepper
- Choice of dressing, to serve

METHOD

- Divide the chicken ham, tomato, carrot, cheddar, and lettuce among 4 tortillas. Season with salt and pepper to taste. Drizzle with your choice of dressing. Roll it up to enclose filling.
- Serve and enjoy.

NUTRITIONAL INFORMATION

Energy	Fat	Carbohydrates	Protein	Sodium
333 calories	11.8 g	26.6 g	30.5 g	354 mg

SAUTEED BEEF AND CORN WRAP

Preparation Time	Total Time	Yield
10 minutes	20 minutes	4 servings

INGREDIENTS

- 2 tablespoons (30 ml) canola oil
- 1/2 cup (30 g) scallions, chopped
- 1 teaspoon (3 g) garlic, minced
- 1 pound (450 g) beef sirloin, ground
- 1 medium (120 g) red bell pepper, cut into thin strips
- 2/3 cup (110 g) sweet corn kernels
- 1 teaspoon (2 g) ground coriander
- 1 teaspoon (2 g) sweet paprika
- 8 (15 g) Romaine lettuce leaves
- 4 (60 g) whole wheat flour tortillas, toasted and warmed
- Salt and freshly ground black pepper
- Choice of dressing, to serve

METHOD

- Heat oil in a non-stick pan or skillet over medium-high flame. Stir-fry scallions and garlic for 2 minutes.
- Add the ground beef and cook for 5 minutes or until browned.
- Add the bell pepper, corn kernels, coriander, and paprika. Cook, stirring often for 5-7 minutes. Season with salt and pepper. Remove from heat and cool slightly.
- Divide the beef mixture among 4 tortillas. Top with

lettuce. Roll it up to enclose filling.

- Serve and enjoy.

NUTRITIONAL INFORMATION

Energy	Fat	Carbohydrates	Protein	Sodium
338 calories	14.6 g	22.4 g	29.8 g	211 mg

MINCED MEAT AND VEGGIE WRAP

Preparation Time	Total Time	Yield
10 minutes	20 minutes	4 servings

INGREDIENTS

- 2 tablespoons (30 ml) canola oil
- 2 shallots (about 40 g each), chopped
- 1 teaspoon (3 g) garlic, finely chopped
- 1 pound (450 g) beef sirloin, minced
- 3/4 cup (185 g) tomato sauce
- 2 teaspoons (10 ml) Worcestershire sauce
- 2 tablespoons (7 g) fresh thyme, chopped
- 8 (15 g) iceberg lettuce leaves
- 1 cup (150 g) cherry tomatoes, quartered
- 4 (60 g) whole wheat flour tortillas, toasted and warmed
- Choice of dressing, to serve
- Salt and freshly ground black pepper

METHOD

- Heat oil in a non-stick pan or skillet over medium-high flame. Stir-fry shallots and garlic for 2 minutes.
- Add the minced beef and cook for 5 minutes or until browned.
- Add the tomato sauce, Worcestershire sauce, and thyme; cook, stirring often for another 5-7 minutes. Season with salt and pepper. Remove from heat and cool slightly.
- Divide the beef mixture among 4 tortillas. Top with

lettuce and tomatoes. Roll it up to enclose filling.

- Serve and enjoy.

NUTRITIONAL INFORMATION

Energy	Fat	Carbohydrates	Protein	Sodium
370 calories	16.4 g	28.9 g	30.6 g	466 mg

TABBOULEH SALAD AND SALMON WRAP

Preparation Time	Total Time	Yield
10 minutes	10 minutes	4 servings

INGREDIENTS

- 2 cups (370 g) prepared Tabbouleh salad
- 4 ounces (125 g) smoked salmon, sliced thinly into strips
- 8 (15 g) Romaine lettuce leaves
- 4 (60 g) pita bread, toasted and warmed
- Salt and freshly ground black pepper

METHOD

- Divide Tabbouleh salad among 4 warmed pita bread. Top with lettuce and smoked salmon. Season with salt and pepper. Roll it up to enclose filling.
- Serve and enjoy.

NUTRITIONAL INFORMATION

Energy	Fat	Carbohydrates	Protein	Sodium
223 calories	5.1 g	32.6 g	11.6 g	707 mg

TUNA SPINACH AND CORN WRAP

Preparation Time	Total Time	Yield
10 minutes	10 minutes	4 servings

INGREDIENTS

- 1 cup (150 g) canned tuna, drained and flaked
- 1/2 cup (85 g) sweetcorn kernels
- 1 cup (30 g) baby spinach
- 1/2 cup (125 g) light mayonnaise
- 2 tablespoons (30 ml) lemon juice
- 1/4 cup (15 g) green onions, chopped
- 4 (60 g) whole wheat flour tortillas, toasted and warmed
- Salt and freshly ground black pepper

METHOD

- In a medium bowl, combine the tuna, sweetcorn, mayonnaise, lemon juice, and green onions. Season with salt and pepper.
- Divide the tuna-spinach mixture among 4 tortillas. Roll it up to enclose filling.
- Serve and enjoy.

NUTRITIONAL INFORMATION

Energy	Fat	Carbohydrates	Protein	Sodium
256 calories	8.5 g	28.6 g	16.0 g	499 mg

TURKEY AND LETTUCE SALAD WRAP

Preparation Time	Total Time	Yield
10 minutes	10 minutes	4 servings

INGREDIENTS

- 1/2 cup (125 g) sour cream
- 1 (40 g) shallot, chopped
- 2 tablespoons (7 g) fresh parsley, chopped
- 8 oz. (250 g) turkey ham, sliced thinly
- 2 (125 g) tomatoes, sliced thinly
- 1 cup (30 g) arugula or baby rocket leaves
- 4 (60 g) whole wheat flour tortillas, toasted and warmed

METHOD

- Combine the sour cream, shallot, and parsley in a small bowl.
- Divide sour cream among 4 tortillas. Spread on one side and then top with turkey ham, tomato slices, and arugula. Roll it up to enclose filling. Cut each into 3-4 slices.
- Serve and enjoy.

NUTRITIONAL INFORMATION

Energy	Fat	Carbohydrates	Protein	Sodium
297 calories	12.8 g	26.9 g	13.8 g	695 mg

TURKEY HAM AND FRESH VEGGIE POCKET

Preparation Time	Total Time	Yield
10 minutes	10 minutes	4 servings

INGREDIENTS

- 8 ounces (250 g) turkey ham, thinly sliced
- 2 medium tomatoes (about 125 g each), thinly sliced
- 1 medium (200 g) cucumber, thinly sliced
- 8 (15 g) Romaine lettuce leaves
- 4 (45 g) pita pockets, toasted and warmed

Honey-Mustard Sauce:

- 1/4 cup (60 g) light mayonnaise
- 2 tablespoons (30 g) Dijon mustard
- 1 tablespoon (20 ml) honey
- 1 tablespoon (15 ml) lemon juice

METHOD

- Mix together mayonnaise, mustard, honey, and lemon juice in a small bowl. Set aside.
- Divide the turkey, tomato, cucumber, and lettuce among 4 pita pockets. Drizzle with prepared honey-mustard sauce.
- Serve and enjoy.

NUTRITIONAL INFORMATION

Energy	Fat	Carbohydrates	Protein	Sodium
289 calories	4.9 g	44.2 g	15.7 g	874 mg

CHICKEN AVOCADO AND CUCUMBER WRAP

Preparation Time	Total Time	Yield
10 minutes	10 minutes	4 servings

INGREDIENTS

- 8 ounces (250 g) roasted chicken breast fillet, thinly sliced
- 1 medium (200 g) avocado, thinly sliced
- 1 medium (125 g) tomato, thinly sliced
- 1 medium (200 g) cucumber, thinly sliced
- 2 tablespoons (7 g) fresh chives, chopped
- 4 (20 g) Romaine lettuce leaves
- 4 (60 g) whole wheat flour tortillas, toasted and warmed
- Choice of dressing, to serve

METHOD

- Divide the chicken, avocado, tomato, cucumber, chives, and lettuce among 4 warmed tortillas. Drizzle with your choice of dressing. Roll it up to enclose filling.
- Serve and enjoy.

NUTRITIONAL INFORMATION

Energy	Fat	Carbohydrates	Protein	Sodium
308 calories	14.2 g	29.0 g	18.0 g	174 mg

TURKEY HAM VEGGIE AND CHEESE WRAP

Preparation Time	Total Time	Yield
10 minutes	10 minutes	4 servings

INGREDIENTS

- 4 ounces (125 g) turkey ham, sliced thinly
- 2 medium tomatoes (about 125 g each), sliced thinly
- 1 medium (110 g) red onion, sliced thinly
- 4 ounces (125 g) cheddar cheese, sliced thinly
- 8 (15 g) Romaine lettuce leaves
- 4 (60 g) flour tortillas, toasted and warmed
- Choice of dressing, to serve

METHOD

- Divide the turkey, tomato, onion, cheese, and lettuce among 4 tortillas. Drizzle with your choice of dressing. Roll it up to enclose filling.
- Serve and enjoy.

NUTRITIONAL INFORMATION

Energy	Fat	Carbohydrates	Protein	Sodium
267 calories	13.1 g	22.5 g	15.2 g	630 mg

VEGETARIAN SANDWICH WRAP

Preparation Time	Total Time	Yield
10 minutes	10 minutes	4 servings

INGREDIENTS

- 2 medium tomatoes (about 125 g each), sliced thinly
- 1 medium (120 g) red bell pepper, sliced thinly
- 1 medium (120 g) yellow bell pepper, sliced thinly
- 1 medium (110 g) red onion, sliced thinly
- 1 medium (200 g) cucumber, sliced thinly
- 1 cup (220 g) cottage cheese
- 4 (60 g) whole wheat flour tortillas, toasted and warmed

Yogurt-Parsley Dressing:

- 6 ounces (185 g) Greek yogurt
- 1 tablespoon (30 ml) lemon juice
- 2 tablespoons (7 g) fresh parsley, chopped
- 1 clove (3 g) garlic, minced
- Salt and freshly ground black pepper

METHOD

- Combine the yogurt, lemon juice, parsley, and garlic in a small bowl. Season with salt and pepper. Mix well.
- Divide the tomatoes, bell peppers, onion, and cucumber among 4 tortillas. Top with cottage cheese and drizzle with yogurt dressing. Roll it up to enclose filling.
- Serve and enjoy.

NUTRITIONAL INFORMATION

Energy	Fat	Carbohydrates	Protein	Sodium
234 calories	7.3 g	32.7 g	19.3 g	378 mg

CHICKEN HAM AND VEGETABLE WRAP

Preparation Time	Total Time	Yield
10 minutes	10 minutes	4 servings

INGREDIENTS

- 8 ounces (250 g) chicken ham, sliced thinly
- 1 medium (200 g) cucumber, sliced thinly
- 1 medium (125 g) tomato, sliced thinly
- 1 medium (110 g) red onion, sliced thinly
- 8 (15 g) Romaine lettuce leaves
- 4 (60 g) flour tortillas, toasted and warmed
- Choice of dressing, to serve

METHOD

- Divide the chicken ham, cucumber, tomato, onion, and lettuce among 4 tortillas. Drizzle with your choice of dressing. Roll it up to enclose filling.
- Serve and enjoy.

NUTRITIONAL INFORMATION

Energy	Fat	Carbohydrates	Protein	Sodium
203 calories	2.9 g	29.4 g	19.0 g	581 mg

CRAB CAKE AND VEGGIE WRAP WITH TARTAR SAUCE

Preparation Time	Total Time	Yield
10 minutes	10 minutes	4 servings

INGREDIENTS

- 4 (2 oz. or 60 g) crab cakes, ready-to-cook
- 1 medium (125 g) tomato, sliced thinly
- 1 medium (110 g) red onion, sliced thinly
- 1 medium (200 g) cucumber, sliced thinly
- 8 (20 g) Romaine lettuce leaves
- 4 (60 g) whole wheat flour tortillas, toasted and warmed

Tartar Sauce:

- 1/2 cup (125 g) light mayonnaise
- 1 teaspoon (2 g) dill weed, chopped
- 1 ½ tablespoon (5 g) fresh chives, finely chopped
- 1 tablespoon (15 g) pickle relish
- 1 teaspoon (5 g) Dijon mustard
- 1 teaspoon (5 ml) hot sauce
- 1 teaspoon (5 ml) Worcestershire sauce

METHOD

- Preheat and set your griddle to high.
- Make the tartar sauce by mixing together mayonnaise, dill, chives, pickle relish, mustard, hot sauce, and Worcestershire sauce in a small bowl. Cover the sauce and keep in the fridge until serving time.

- Grill the crab cakes until cooked through, about 3-4 minutes on each side. Remove from the heat and transfer to a chopping board. Cut into small pieces.
- Divide the crab cakes, cucumber, tomato, onion, and lettuce among 4 warmed tortillas. Drizzle with prepared tartar sauce. Roll it up to enclose filling.
- Serve and enjoy.

NUTRITIONAL INFORMATION

Energy	Fat	Carbohydrates	Protein	Sodium
342 calories	14.9 g	42.2 g	15.0 g	655 mg

TUNA AND RADISH SALAD WRAP

Preparation Time	Total Time	Yield
10 minutes	10 minutes	4 servings

INGREDIENTS

- 1/2 cup (125 g) light mayonnaise
- 1 (60 g) celery stalk, chopped
- 2 tablespoons (7 g) fresh parsley, chopped
- 1 tablespoon (15 g) pickle relish
- 6 ounces (185 g) canned tuna in water, drained and flaked
- Salt and freshly ground black pepper
- 1 cup (120 g) radish, sliced thinly
- 1 medium (110 g) onion, sliced thinly
- 2 cups (60 g) baby spinach
- 4 (60 g) flour tortillas, toasted and warmed

METHOD

- Mix together mayonnaise, celery, parsley, pickle relish, and tuna in a medium bowl. Season with salt and pepper.
- Divide the spinach, radish, and onion among 4 warmed tortillas. Top with tuna salad mixture. Roll it up to enclose filling.
- Serve and enjoy.

NUTRITIONAL INFORMATION

Energy	Fat	Carbohydrates	Protein	Sodium
350 calories	14.7 g	39.1 g	17.4 g	515 mg

TURKEY AND EGG AND CHEESE PINWHEELS

Preparation Time	Total Time	Yield
15 minutes	15 minutes	4 servings

INGREDIENTS

- 2 (60 g) hard-boiled eggs
- 1/2 cup (125 g) light mayonnaise
- 1 (40 g) shallot, chopped
- 1 tablespoon (15 g) pickle relish
- 1 teaspoon (3 g) garlic, minced
- Salt and freshly ground black pepper
- 4 ounces (125 g) turkey ham, sliced thinly
- 4 (60 g) flour tortillas, toasted and warmed

METHOD

- In a medium bowl, mix together eggs, mayonnaise, shallot, pickle relish, and garlic. Season with salt and pepper.
- Divide the egg mixture and turkey ham among 4 warmed tortillas. Roll it up to enclose filling. Cut into 4 slices crosswise and hold each pinwheel with a toothpick.
- Serve and enjoy.

NUTRITIONAL INFORMATION

Energy	Fat	Carbohydrates	Protein	Sodium
322 calories	16.9 g	30.1 g	11.5 g	893 mg

CHICKEN CHEESE AND LETTUCE PINWHEELS

Preparation Time	Total Time	Yield
10 minutes	10 minutes	4 servings

INGREDIENTS

- 1 ½ cups (210 g) cooked chicken breast, shredded
- 1/2 cup (125 g) light mayonnaise
- 1/4 cup (15 g) green onions, chopped
- 2 tablespoons (30 g) Dijon mustard
- 1 tablespoon (15 g) pickle relish
- Salt and freshly ground black pepper
- 4 (1 oz. or 30 g) cheddar cheese slices
- 8 (15 g) Romaine lettuce leaves
- 4 (60 g) flour tortillas, toasted and warmed

METHOD

- In a medium bowl, mix together chicken, mayonnaise, green onions, mustard, and pickle relish. Season with salt and pepper.
- Divide the chicken mixture among 4 warmed tortillas. Top with cheese and lettuce leaves. Roll it up to enclose filling. Cut into 4 slices crosswise.
- Serve and enjoy.

NUTRITIONAL INFORMATION

Energy	Fat	Carbohydrates	Protein	Sodium
365 calories	18.4 g	29.7 g	24.5 g	722 mg

TURKEY AND SPINACH SALAD WRAP

Preparation Time	Total Time	Yield
10 minutes	10 minutes	4 servings

INGREDIENTS

- 1/4 cup (60 ml) olive oil
- 3 tablespoons (45 ml) balsamic vinegar
- 1/4 teaspoon (0.5 g) dried oregano
- 1/4 teaspoon (0.5 g) dried rosemary
- 1 cup (150 g) cherry tomatoes, halved
- 1 medium (110 g) red onion, sliced thinly
- 2 cups (60 g) baby spinach
- 4 (1 oz. or 30 g) turkey ham, sliced thinly
- 4 (60 g) flour tortillas, toasted and warmed

METHOD

- Whisk together olive oil, balsamic vinegar, oregano, and rosemary in a medium bowl. Season with salt and pepper.
- Add the cherry tomatoes, onion, and spinach. Toss to combine well.
- Divide the spinach salad among 4 warmed tortillas. Top with turkey ham. Roll it up to enclose filling.
- Serve and enjoy.

NUTRITIONAL INFORMATION

Energy	Fat	Carbohydrates	Protein	Sodium
297 calories	16.1 g	11.9 g	11.9 g	329 mg

HERBED CHICKEN AND AVOCADO WRAP

Preparation Time	Total Time	Yield
10 minutes	10 minutes	4 servings

INGREDIENTS

- 4 (3 oz. or 85 g) grilled chicken fillet with herbs, cut into strips
- 1 medium (200 g) avocado, stoned and sliced thinly
- 1 medium (120 g) yellow bell pepper, sliced thinly into strips
- 1/2 cup (125 g) prepared salsa
- 4 (60 g) whole wheat flour tortillas, toasted and warmed

METHOD

- Divide the grilled herbed chicken among 4 warmed tortillas. Top with avocado, bell pepper, and salsa. Roll it up to enclose filling.
- Serve and enjoy.

NUTRITIONAL INFORMATION

Energy	Fat	Carbohydrates	Protein	Sodium
325 calories	14.4 g	32.6 g	23.8 g	328 mg

CHILI BEEF AND BEAN WRAP

Preparation Time	Total Time	Yield
10 minutes	25 minutes	4 servings

INGREDIENTS

- 1 pound (450 g) lean beef, minced
- 2 tablespoons (30 ml) olive oil
- 2 teaspoons (6 g) garlic, chopped
- 1 medium (110 g) onion, chopped
- 1 cup (250 g) canned refried beans
- 1 teaspoon (1 g) red hot chili pepper, chopped
- 1 teaspoon (1 g) sweet paprika
- 2 tablespoons (7 g) fresh cilantro, chopped
- Kosher salt and freshly ground black pepper
- 4 (60 g) whole wheat flour tortillas, toasted and warmed

METHOD

- In a large non-stick pan, add 1 tablespoon oil, and heat over medium-high flame. Cook the minced beef until browned. Then, transfer to a clean plate. Set aside.
- In the same pan, put the remaining 1 tablespoon oil and heat over medium-high flame. Add the onion and garlic; cook, stirring until fragrant, about 2-3 minutes.
- Stir in refried beans, chili pepper, and paprika. Cook for 5 minutes.
- Next, add the minced beef along with the cilantro; cook, stirring further 5 minutes. Season to taste. Remove from heat and cool slightly.

- Divide the beef mixture among 4 warmed tortillas. Roll it up to enclose filling.
- Serve and enjoy.

NUTRITIONAL INFORMATION

Energy	Fat	Carbohydrates	Protein	Sodium
414 calories	16.5 g	30.7 g	36.8 g	447 mg

CRAB AND CORN SALAD WRAP

Preparation Time	Total Time	Yield
10 minutes	10 minutes	4 servings

INGREDIENTS

- 8 pcs. Kani or imitation crab sticks, diced
- 1 cup (175 g) canned sweetcorn kernels
- 1/2 cup (65 g) carrot, chopped
- 1 medium (200 g) cucumber, chopped
- 1 medium (110 g) red onion, chopped
- 1 (60 g) stalk celery, chopped
- 1/2 cup (125 g) Japanese mayonnaise
- 2 tablespoons (30 g) Dijon mustard
- 1 tablespoon (20 ml) honey
- 4 (60 g) whole wheat flour tortillas, toasted and warmed
- Salt and freshly ground black pepper

METHOD

- Whisk together mayonnaise, mustard, and honey in a medium bowl.
- Add the Kani, corn, carrot, cucumber, and celery. Toss to combine well. Season to taste.
- Divide the crab salad among 4 warmed tortillas. Roll it up to enclose filling.
- Serve and enjoy.

NUTRITIONAL INFORMATION

Energy	Fat	Carbohydrates	Protein	Sodium
379 calories	17.0 g	38.4 g	27.8 g	675 mg

CHICKEN APPLE AND CELERY WRAP

Preparation Time	Total Time	Yield
10 minutes	10 minutes	4 servings

INGREDIENTS

- 4 (3 oz. or 85 g) roasted chicken fillet, cut into strips
- 1 medium (185 g) apple, cored and sliced thinly
- 1 stalk (60 g) celery, chopped
- 4 (60 g) whole wheat flour tortillas, toasted and warmed

Lemon-Yogurt Sauce:

- 6 ounces (180 g) Greek yogurt, plain
- 2 tablespoons (30 ml) lemon juice
- 2 tablespoons (30 g) shallot, finely chopped
- 1 tablespoon (3.5 g) fresh parsley, finely chopped

METHOD

- Whisk together all ingredients for the lemon-yogurt sauce in a small bowl. Season with salt and pepper. Set aside.
- Divide the chicken, apple slices, and celery among 4 tortillas. Top with prepared yogurt sauce. Roll it up to enclose filling.
- Serve and enjoy.

NUTRITIONAL INFORMATION

Energy	Fat	Carbohydrates	Protein	Sodium
310 calories	8.7 g	32.0 g	25.0 g	361 mg

EGGPLANT MUSHROOM AND PEPPER WRAP

Preparation Time	Total Time	Yield
10 minutes	25 minutes	4 servings

INGREDIENTS

- 2 tablespoons (30 ml) canola oil
- 1 medium (120 g) onion, sliced thinly
- 1 cup (150 g) button mushrooms, sliced thinly
- 1 large (200 g) eggplant, sliced thinly
- 1 medium (125 g) red bell pepper, sliced thinly
- 1 tablespoon (15 ml) Worcestershire sauce
- 1 tablespoon (15 ml) soy sauce
- 1 tablespoon (15 g) chili garlic sauce
- 1/4 teaspoon (0.5 g) ground coriander
- 1/4 teaspoon (0.5 g) freshly ground black pepper
- 4 (20 g) Romaine lettuce leaves
- 4 (60 g) whole wheat flour tortillas, toasted and warmed

METHOD

- Heat 2 tablespoons oil in a large skillet over medium-high flame. Stir-fry onion for 2-3 minutes.
- Add the mushrooms, eggplant, bell pepper, Worcestershire sauce, soy sauce, and chili garlic sauce. Cook, stirring for 8-10 minutes or until vegetables are tender. Season with coriander and pepper. Remove from heat and cool slightly.
- Divide the lettuce leaves and stir-fried vegetables among 4 warmed tortillas. Roll it up to enclose filling.

- Serve and enjoy.

NUTRITIONAL INFORMATION

Energy	Fat	Carbohydrates	Protein	Sodium
264 calories	10.9 g	36.9 g	6.3 g	465 mg

GRILLED CHICKEN TOMATO AND CHEDDAR WRAP

Preparation Time	Total Time	Yield
10 minutes	10 minutes	4 servings

INGREDIENTS

- 4 (3 oz. or 85 g) grilled chicken fillet, shredded
- 1 medium (125 g) tomato, sliced thinly
- 4 (1 oz. or 30 g) slices cheddar cheese
- 4 tablespoons (60 g) mayonnaise
- 4 (20 g) Romaine lettuce leaves
- 4 (60 g) flour tortillas, toasted and warmed

METHOD

- Spread 1 tablespoon mayonnaise on one side of each tortilla.
- Next, add the lettuce, chicken, tomato, and cheese. Roll it up to enclose filling.
- Serve and enjoy.

NUTRITIONAL INFORMATION

Energy	Fat	Carbohydrates	Protein	Sodium
406 calories	18.4 g	28.7 g	30.3 g	510 mg

MEDITERRANEAN CHICKEN WRAP

Preparation Time	Total Time	Yield
10 minutes	10 minutes	4 servings

INGREDIENTS

- 4 (3 oz. or 85 g) roasted chicken fillet, cut into strips
- 1 cup (150 g) cherry tomatoes, quartered
- 1/2 cup (30 g) fresh basil leaves
- 4 (60 g) flour tortillas, toasted and warmed

Balsamic Vinaigrette:

- 2 tablespoons (30 ml) olive oil
- 2 tablespoons (30 ml) balsamic vinegar
- 1 tablespoon (15 g) Dijon mustard
- 1 tablespoons (20 ml) honey
- 1 tablespoon (3.5 g) fresh parsley, finely chopped
- Salt and freshly ground black pepper

METHOD

- Whisk together all ingredients for the balsamic vinaigrette in a small bowl. Season with salt and pepper. Set aside.
- Divide the chicken strips, cherry tomatoes, and basil among 4 warmed tortillas. Drizzle with balsamic vinaigrette. Roll it up to enclose filling.
- Serve and enjoy.

NUTRITIONAL INFORMATION

Energy	Fat	Carbohydrates	Protein	Sodium
377 calories	12.7 g	25.8 g	31.9 g	378 mg

GRILLED VEGETABLES AND FETA WRAP

Preparation Time	Total Time	Yield
10 minutes	10 minutes	4 servings

INGREDIENTS

- 1 medium (200 g) zucchini, sliced thinly
- 1 medium (200 g) eggplant, sliced thinly
- 1 medium (125 g) tomato, sliced thinly
- 1 medium (120 g) onion, sliced thinly
- 1 cup (150 g) herbed feta cheese, crumbled
- 4 (60 g) whole wheat flour tortillas, toasted and warmed
- Salt and freshly ground black pepper
- Cooking oil spray

Lemon Vinaigrette with Honey:

- 2 tablespoons (30 ml) olive oil
- 2 tablespoons (30 ml) lemon juice
- 1 tablespoon (20 ml) honey
- 1 tablespoon (3.5 g) fresh parsley, finely chopped

METHOD

- Preheat and set your grill or griddle to high. Lightly grease with oil spray.
- Whisk together all ingredients for the lemon vinaigrette in a small bowl. Season with salt and pepper. Set aside.
- Season vegetable slices with salt and pepper. Grill for 7-10 minutes or until tender and grill marks form. Remove from heat.
- Divide the grilled vegetables among 4 warmed tortillas.

Top with feta cheese and drizzle with prepared lemon vinaigrette. Roll it up to enclose filling.
- Serve and enjoy.

NUTRITIONAL INFORMATION

Energy	Fat	Carbohydrates	Protein	Sodium
384 calories	21.8 g	41.1 g	8.9 g	415 mg

CHICKEN AND MUSHROOM IN LETTUCE WRAP

Preparation Time	Total Time	Yield
10 minutes	20 minutes	6 servings

INGREDIENTS

- 2 tablespoons (30 ml) canola oil
- 2 cloves (6 g) garlic, minced
- 1 medium (110 g) red onion, chopped
- 1 pound (450 g) chicken breast fillet, minced
- 1 cup (150 g) button mushrooms, chopped
- 1 tablespoon (7 g) fresh cilantro, chopped
- 2 tablespoons (30 ml) oyster sauce
- 1 teaspoon (5 ml) Worcestershire sauce
- 1 small head (about 350 g) lettuce, leaves separated
- Kosher salt and freshly ground black pepper

METHOD

- In a non-stick pan or skillet, add 2 tablespoons oil and heat over medium-high flame. Cook chopped onion and garlic, stirring often for 3 minutes.
- Add the minced chicken; cook, stirring often until browned.
- Add the chopped mushrooms, cilantro, oyster sauce, and Worcestershire sauce. Season to taste. Cook further 3-5 minutes, stirring occasionally. Remove from heat and cool slightly.

- Take 2 tablespoons of chicken mixture and place in the middle of each lettuce leaf; then, slightly fold to enclose filling.
- Place in a serving dish and repeat procedure for the remaining chicken mixture.
- Serve and enjoy.

NUTRITIONAL INFORMATION

Energy	Fat	Carbohydrates	Protein	Sodium
151 calories	6.8 g	5.5 g	16.9 g	99 mg

MINCED BEEF AND VEGGIES IN LETTUCE WRAP

Preparation Time	Total Time	Yield
10 minutes	25 minutes	6 servings

INGREDIENTS

- 2 tablespoons (30 ml) canola oil
- 2 shallots (about 40 g each), chopped
- 1 teaspoon (3 g) garlic, minced
- 1 pound (450 g) beef sirloin, minced
- 1 medium (60 g) carrot, chopped
- 1 cup (150 g) button mushroom, chopped
- 1 stalk (60 g) celery, chopped
- 2 tablespoons (30 g) oyster sauce
- 1 teaspoon (5 ml) Worcestershire sauce
- 1 small head (350 g) lettuce, leaves separated
- 1/4 cup (15 g) fresh chives, chopped
- Salt and freshly ground black pepper

METHOD

- Add oil in a large non-stick pan or skillet and place over medium-high flame. Stir-fry shallots and garlic until fragrant, about 2-3 minutes.
- Stir in minced meat and cook until browned, about 5 minutes.
- Add the carrot, mushroom, celery, oyster sauce, and Worcestershire sauce. Season with salt and pepper

to taste. Cook further 5 minutes, stirring occasionally. Remove from heat and cool slightly.
- Spoon 2 tablespoons beef mixture and place in the middle of each lettuce leaf. Sprinkle with chives. Slightly fold to enclose filling. Repeat with remaining lettuce and beef mixture.
- Serve and enjoy.

NUTRITIONAL INFORMATION

Energy	Fat	Carbohydrates	Protein	Sodium
171 calories	8.4 g	5.6 g	18.1 g	201 mg

QUICK AND EASY VEGAN WRAP

Preparation Time	Total Time	Yield
10 minutes	10 minutes	4 servings

INGREDIENTS

- 1 medium (200 g) cucumber, cut into thin strips
- 1 medium (125 g) tomato, cut into thin strips
- 1 medium (120 g) red bell pepper, cut into thin strips
- 1 medium (120 g) yellow bell pepper, cut into thin strips
- 2 tablespoons (30 ml) olive oil
- 2 tablespoons (30 ml) lime juice
- 1 small head (350 g) lettuce, leaves separated
- Salt and ground black pepper

METHOD

- Place the cucumber, tomato, and pepper strips in a medium bowl.
- Drizzle with olive oil and lime juice. Season with salt and pepper to taste. Toss to combine well.
- Serve veggie strips wrapped in lettuce leaves.
- Enjoy.

NUTRITIONAL INFORMATION

Energy	Fat	Carbohydrates	Protein	Sodium
155 calories	14.3 g	8.4 g	1.4 g	170 mg

MIXED FRUITS AND COTTAGE CHEESE WRAP WITH ALMONDS

Preparation Time	Total Time	Yield
10 minutes	10 minutes	4 servings

INGREDIENTS

- 1 cup (250 g) cottage cheese, crumbled
- 1 cup (150 g) mixed berries
- 1 medium (150 g) peach, sliced thinly
- 1 medium (80 g) kiwifruit, sliced thinly
- 4 teaspoons (30 ml) honey
- 4 tablespoons (30 g) slivered almonds
- 4 (60 g) flour tortillas, toasted and warmed

METHOD

- Divide the cottage among 4 warmed tortillas. Top with mixed berries, peach, and kiwi slices. Drizzle with honey. Sprinkle with almonds. Roll it up to enclose filling.
- Serve and enjoy.